1 MONTH OF
FREE
READING

at

www.ForgottenBooks.com

By purchasing this book you are eligible for one month membership to ForgottenBooks.com, giving you unlimited access to our entire collection of over 1,000,000 titles via our web site and mobile apps.

To claim your free month visit:

www.forgottenbooks.com/free231767

ISBN 978-0-483-80776-1
PIBN 10231767

SONGS

OF THE

SHAWANGUNKS.

BY

RALCY H. BELL.

SONGS AND FRAGMENTS OF THE SHAWANGUNKS.

BY RALCY H. BELL.

And men are only fragments
  Of a passion ever young;
And life is only throbbings
  Of the hot breath of the Sun;
And death is but an ebb-tide
  Or the pulseless bride of night.

DEDICATION.

                                    MEREDITH.

To one who has been foremost in my consider-
ations of respect and esteem for years — my friend
and much more — to whom I owe, in great part,
my high appreciation of the beautiful — the ideal —
and love for that which becomes it; who has
flecked my life with rapturous dreams of Joy, and
tuned her soul responsively in accord with mine
when our "hearts palpitated as if they contained
but a single soul;" who has tirelessly ministered to
my changing moods, earnestly joined in my pleas-
ures and wept for my woes, I affectionately ascribe
this unworthy gift ; *and*

"*If I, by the Throne, should behold her,**
Smiling up with those eyes loved so well,
Close, close in my arms I would fold her,*
And drop with her* down to Sweet Hell !"

**You in the original ; from "Poems of Passion," by Ella Wheeler Wilcox —
the sweetest and brainiest poet of this age.*

UNITED STATES SENATE,
COMMITTEE ON THE DISTRICT OF COLUMBIA.

WASHINGTON, D. C., Aug. 21, 1890.

DEAR MR. BELL:

In reply to yours of 14th inst. I would say that my impression would be that you will receive greater advantage from publishing your book on your own account than in the usual method, through agents and newspaper companies.

I thank you for your personal suggestions in connection with your work.

Very truly yours,

Jno. J. Ingalls

MR. R. H. BELL,
Rosendale, N. Y.

PREFACE.

I have dreamed a few dreams in the lap of Nature ; at leisure I have written little verses in which I have painted some of my " dreams and memories with words."

I have wandered whither my thoughts have led, governed by the same law, may be, that shapes the course of brooks or gives to the wind its various and viewless paths. Guide-boards and beaten roads have not been regarded, but I have found a consolation, sometimes, in the foot-prints of others — a prophecy. These verses were not written for the scholar, nor to teach ; most of them are commemorative.

I shall feel satisfied if this little volume interests *those* of my friends at whose solicitation it was published.

R. H. B.

" *But all subsists by elemental strife*
And passions are the elements of life,
The general order since the whole began,
Is kept in nature and is kept in man."

———

* * * Everything except truth wears, and needs to wear, a mask. Little souls are ashamed of Nature. Prudery pretends to have only those passions that it cannot feel. Moral poetry is like a respectable canal that never overflows its banks. It has weirs through which, slowly and without damage, any excess of feeling is allowed to flow. It makes excuses for nature, and regards love as an interesting convict. * * * Art creates, combines, and reveals. It is the highest manifestation of thought, of passion, of love, of intuition. It is the highest form of expression, of history and prophecy. It allows us to look at an unmasked soul, to fathom the abysses of passion ; to understand the heights and depths of love. * * * The nude in art has rendered holy the beauty of woman. Every Greek statue pleads for mothers and sisters. From these marbles come strains of music. They have filled the heart of man with tenderness and worship. They have kindled reverence, admiration and love. * * * The prudent is not the poetic ; it is the mathematical. Genius is the spirit of abandon ; it is joyous, irresponsible. It moves in the swell and curve of billows ; it is careless of conduct and consequence.

"ART AND MORALITY"—R. G. INGERSOLL.

WORDS OF ACKNOWLEDGMENT.

To Reuben D. Slater, the artist, whose culture and kindness, genius and manhood have made me his friend; to A. V. Haight, the printer, whose character and skill have won my admiration; and to Cornelius I. Lefever, of Rosendale, N. Y., whose candor and courage, liberality, and width and depth of brain and heart, and whose loyal friendship has made me his everlasting friend, I gratefully acknowledge their encouragement and assistance.

R. H. B.

LIST OF ILLUSTRATIONS.

INDEX.

SONGS

OF THE

SHAWANGUNKS.

IMMORTALITY.

Fair Hope was wed to Passion —
    A lover bold and strong —
And Hope was rich in beauty,
    And Passion rich in song.

They met and loved at morning ;
    They loved and wed at noon,
For the joys they sought are fleeting,
    And night comes all too soon.

They made them a bed of roses
    And hid beneath their bloom ;
And bathed themselves in dew-drops,
    And in a rose perfume.

For Hope was coy and bashful,
    'Neath blushes hid her face ;
While Passion, bold and eager,
    Clasp'd Hope in his embrace.

They fed on dreams of rapture,
    On transports fierce and wild,
And Immortality was,
    To them, their first-born child.

THROUGH MISTS OF MEMORY.

*" * * A flowing tide that wandered back*
Along the course and valley of the past."

I wandered oft in dreamy years gone by
On ground forbidden — known to none save I.
It was a fair and flow'ry gemmèd belt
Where sylvan beauty grew, and sweet love dwelt ;
Where purest pleasure found her happy mate
And hours of wingèd joy flew by in state
Of listless glee, unheeded till too late
Where priceless treasures, plucked with careless ease
Now serves but to intensify and tease
The exiled heart, — in throes of hopeless thrall,—
Encompassed round by seas of bitter gall.

O, happy, blissful land of heavenly joy
That won the heart and kept the ardent boy
From dens of vice and thoughts of crafty gain ;
That saved his boat from shoals and bars of pain !
Full oft I wandered o'er its flow'ry mead
'Neath dreamy spells, and charms of love's sweet
    need,

Full oft I strayed along each sacred dell
And stoop'd to sip from springs of magic spell
Divinest nectar, drank by gods of love
Alone ; and wooed to rest on hills above
"Where perfect peace finds perfect form," and
   Sleep —
Calm Goddess—tranquilly enfolds to keep
Her ward from harm of Fear and frightful dreams ;
Not e'en her rustling garments flow between
The sleeper's rest and his unconsciousness.

O, dreamy child of Fate ! poor wand'ring brook
'Mid hills and dales of circumstance ! nor look,
Nor calculate thy speed, nor course, nor be
Thy journey marked nor map'd, for to the sea
Must wander all the streams.   Then why disturb
Thy bosom with a care ; or seek to curb
Thy mental steed's impassioned will, or 'press
Within thy other nature, one caress
Which thou might'st give to flowers, on thy banks,
That bloom all lonely, breathing back their thanks
For one soft touch of passion-cooling dew ?
Poor exile ! driv'n from happy, holy hills,
No more I'll roam and play like joyous rills
About my pretty park.   My life is lean

In pleasure — joyless night — no starry queen
To guide my weary, wand'ring, wayward feet
To soothing rest ; but onward through the heat
Of living hell, o'er coals of discontent
That I must smother, hobble on, nor vent
My untold sorrow, but stray on through drear
And darksome wood of heartless men, where Fear
And Fancy form a thousand sprites that haunt
The trammeled mind, and lure and leer, and daunt
Misguided travelers—toys of Wizard Fate.
I'll taste my pleasures never more ; my dream
Is ended, and the future which did seem
So bright and rich in love, is dim and far,
And all too thick with clouds to show a star.

FLOOD TIDE.

There is nothing so charmful and nothing so blissful,
So filled with sweet thoughts and of transport so
    chock-full,
So full of blue sky and green patches of earth —
Replete with fair heaven and free from all dearth —
So rich and so rare, so perfect, in truth,
As the pleasures of love in the morning of youth.

There is nothing so charmful and nothing so blissful,
So filled with soul-perfume, of sunshine so brim-full,
So full of bird-song, brook-music and mirth,
So full of heart treasure, the purest on earth,
So rosy with hope, resplendent, in truth,
As the pleasures of love in the morning of youth.

There is nothing so cheerful and nothing so fruitful,
So full of fair nature, of words so helpful,
So throbbing with life and with freedom aflame,
So holy, with love, and deserving the name
So bursting with passion, so earnest in truth,
As the pleasures of love in the morning of youth.

O, give me fresh youth in the morning's full prime,
And let all his raptures and pleasures be mine,
At the dawn when the pulse's red torrent s' a-fire,
And the soul is surcharged with the flame of desire;
O, to drink from that cup—that *fountain*, in truth,
Of the pleasures of love in the morning of youth!

It is worth all this life of sorrow and pain,
It is worth all the clouds, the tears and the rain,
It is worth all the winds that Adversity blows,
It is worth all the wrinkles of Age and his snows,
Is this dawn of the manhood, this *flood-tide*, in truth,
Of the pleasures of love in the morning of youth.

CANST THOU TELL ME?

Life is the wave's deep whisper on the shore
Of a great sea beyond.

HENRY ABBEY.

O poet, canst thou tell me what is life —
   This throb and thrill, this brief, uneven way,
   This light and shadow of a summer day,
This calm ennui, this toil, this care and strife
      Of a vague, vague dream?

For death to me is not so strange and vain,
   So filled with barrenness, so cold and drear;
   So void, so desolate, so free from cheer
As joyless life — that moth of passion, pain —
      Broken mid-day beam!

O, what is this eternal ebb and flow,
   This strange and ceaseless breathing of the deep?
   And what these moods; this calm and shaded sleep;
This wondrous tomb wherein we all must go
      To a dreamless dream?

HENRY ABBEY.

O, poet ! O tender-eyed musician ! songs
Which thou hast sung will live when all the wrongs
That man can do to man have died or flown,
Like frightened sprites of darkness at the dawn
Behind the misty curtained ages — past.

Thy gentle strains shall touch the strings of hearts
With magic music — soft æolian sighs,
Sweet breath of love, a musical sadness o' tears,
And all the symphonies that play about
The hearts of human hearts, and kiss and waft
Rich pollen odors, minglingly, as warm
Air softened into zephyrs, sings of love
To flowers, making many one ; so thou
O, Abbey, with thy tender songs unite
Us human flowers into one family,
Wherein the love of goodness and an eye
For beauty are the bonds of brotherhood.

Thy melodies like wooded streams that flow
A little way through sylvan dells and go
All uncomplainingly through shades and beds
Of moss, shall yet bear upon their mirror breasts
The reflex of the stars, and laugh and sing
O'er many a pebbly meadow-course and bring
Upon their billowy bosoms show'rs of bloom —
The blessed tributes of the loving's love —
Unto the fated arms that reach from out
The whence " Where death's impatient deep
Hems in the narrow continent of life."

NAIAD NATRIECE.

There is nothing my soul lacks or misses
As I clasp the dream shape to my breast.
                    ELLA WHEELER WILCOX.

When low the summer sun was set,
    And day gave way to gloom,
I sat one evening 'neath a tree,
    And wove at Fancy's loom :
The warp and woof of pictured dreams ;
    The weft was strange to see,
Through sights and thoughts a-drifting by
    And floating over me.

Soft breezes low came bearing out
    From many a perfumed dell,
The scented breath of sleeping flowers
    More sweet than I can tell.
A-musing there, alone I sat,
    Surrounded by a dream ;
A-listening to the forest sighs
    And music of a stream.

I spied a form whose perfect mould
    Showed plain against the shade ;
The curving bust, the sculptured arms,
    Bespoke a naked maid.
Her hair was long and dark as night,
    While she was fair as day,
And blended soft on either cheek
    A rosy bloom of May.

"O maid !" I cried, "O queen of love !
    O forest beauty fair !
Come, twine me in thy shapely arms,
    And hide me with thy hair.
And take me gently on thy breast,
    Upon thy bosom bare,
And on those billows let me rest,
    Serene from toil and care."

A startled look the maiden took,
    This forest naiad fair,
And trembling like a frightened fawn
    The night-wind tosst her hair.
The startled look the maiden took
    Gave way to deep surprise,
But from her soul of heat and truth
    A love-light filled her eyes.

Then reaching forth she took my hand,
  And led me through the wood,
To where a pretty Naiad band
  Waist deep in water stood ;
And some were combing out their hair,
  And some a-bathing seemed,
While all so sweet, divinely fair,
  Half made me think I dreamed.

And some were blonds and some brunettes,
  And all supreme of mould ;
Though all were naked, all were dresst,
  With modesty tenfold.
" My sisters dear, my lover here,"
  Began this sweet Natriece,
" I brought that thou mayst see me wed
  A son of ancient Greece."

Then 'round about in mirthful glee,
  They swarmed in rapturous bliss,
And presst upon my burning cheek
  Full many an honest kiss.
And all the nobler charms and trills
  A virtuous woman blesses,
In spend-thrift glee were given to me,
  In wild-wood hugs and kisses.

And ere the trembling bars of gray
  Foretold the coming morn,
Our marriage bed was made of moss,
  A child to us was born.
And we were wed on a mossy bed,
  The Morning star was our priest ;
And bless the time that made her mine !
  And bless our wedding feast.

And this is why I love so well
  The wild-wood and the streams ;
And this is why I love to tell
  In wild-wood song my dreams.
For Nature is my loving wife ;
  To her I'm doubly bound
With ties of kin and links of love,
  And trees and flow'rs around.

LOVE'S APPEAL.

What is title? What is treasure?
  What is reputation's care?
If we lead a life of pleasure,
  'Tis no matter how nor where.

    *   *   *

Does the train attended carriage
  Through the country lighter rove?
Does the sober bed of marriage
  Witness brighter scenes of love?

ROBERT BURNS.

The mountain brooklets mingle
  With neighboring low-land streams;
And the sun of heaven brightens
  The lone moon's silver beams.

The sun and earth are mingled;
  Their transports spring the flowers;
And the dews of meadows mingle
  In ecstasy with showers.

The twilight weds the morning;
  And morning kisses night;

Oft the lowest wed the highest
  And keep the balance right.

The clouds embrace the mountains,
  And the mountains pierce the blue ;
For as all things mingle ever,
  Then why not I with you ?

The circling worlds around us,
  With stars of heaven wed ;
And life complete is never
  'Til joined on marriage bed.

And flowers kiss each other,
  And are wed by the evening dew ;
And the breezes kiss each other,
  Then why not I kiss you ?

And waves embrace each other,
  And climb and clasp the beach ;
And the ivy twines the oak tree ; —
  Thy arms around me reach.

O, precious darling Nellie !
  Come twine thee, sweet, with me,
And remember that your lover,
  Is dying all for thee.

Take lesson, sweet one, truly,
　　From birds and air and dew ;
From the flowers and showers and nature —
　　Come join one soul-love, true !

For earth holds nothing single ;
　　The pure in love can kiss ;
When our loves are true they mingle
　　In sacred flames of bliss.

I pray thee, Nellie darling,
　　Come twine me 'round about
With your dainty snow-white bare arms,
　　And breathe your passion out.

Come break the bonds that bind you
　　To customs of the past,
And we'll live in dreams of rapture ;
　　Enjoy them while they last.

For life at best is fleeting ;
　　And joys take wing too soon,
Why then waste one golden moment
　　'Neath sun-light, stars or moon ?

'Tis false, nor wisdom teaches
　　That sacrifice is right ;

And *nobility* ne'er asks it—
  Reverse deserves no mite.

*   *   *

Forgive me, love, I pray thee,
  For the love we dare not speak ;
Nor deem it wrong my darling
  That I prize this gem I seek.

The human heart is boundless,
  And love must ever dwell
With the heart that holds its magnet,
  Nor *how* nor *why* can tell.

I only know I love you
  With a love that's half divine ;
The pure, sweet face of Nellie
  In my soul must ever shine.

" How long," do you ask, " will I love you ? "
  As long as the seasons roll ;
As long as the flowers love sunshine ;
  .As long as the life of my soul.

PROTEUS PASSION.

O, joyful is the land of love,
    And blissful are her sun-lit aisles,
And happy are congenial hearts
    By Passion clothed and fed on smiles.

And happy they whose parting lips
    In kisses pay the toll of love,
With dewy sweets and heavenly sips
    On "Th' dear warm mouth of those we love.'

For life is fed by Passion's flame —
    From Passion's heat endures the rust
And moth of time — but starves and dies
    When passion pales, and sinks to dust.

And cold and drear would be the world,
    Nor warmth nor nurture here be found
For bursting bud and blooming flow'r
    If Passion's lamps were not hung 'round.

Though Passion is a Proteus thing,
    And takes at times the serpent's sting,
It dons again the painted wing
    And writes the songs that mortals sing

Upon the very air we breathe.
  It gives us strength and feeds our heart
Upon the blessed dreams of Hope —
  Or kills us with its piercing dart.

NOCTU.

" The month was in the downward year."

The hoary locks of Winter Time has shook,
And from their folds the ground is silvered o'er,
And ev'ry gaping nook has been supplied
From mines exhaustless; All the crystal gems,
And flow'rs and starry forms from viewless depths,
Like rarest gems of men, unsought are found
If found at all.   The Earth, a fav'rite bride
Of Sol, upon her bed of cloud has turned
To take a nap.   Her first harsh breath of sleep
Now rasps the chilly air; her chamber dome
Of azure, decked with heavens diamonds
Is draped with not a fleecy white nor gauze
Of mist; and through the window of the sky
The Moon, a crescent bark that rides and roves
A vasty deep unknown to man, is seen
To dip her silver prow behind the wave
Of some far distant hill and drop from out
Of sight.   The shadows deepen and the night
Grows cold and drear; the year of Ninety's now
So old that scarcely fifteen days shall come

And go before he's laid within the grave
That all the years gone by have dug, and all
The future years will cover deep with dust —
A lonely grave within a desert wierd —
That awful, lonesome grave-yard called THE PAST,
Whereon no stone is set, no crumbling pile
To mark forgotten graves ; whereof there is
No need ; No human soul did ever roam
That boundless waste, nor any living thing
Has ever there found way — a pathless world
Wherein there is no voice, no sound nor sigh,
No song, no joy nor pain, no rain of tears —
Oblivion, the darkness of the dead,
Is king ; Equality-in-dust, the queen ;
They reign supreme, alone, alone, alone.

The trees upon the mountain's northern side,
Along which winds this road I tread to-night
To see my blessed Queen of Queens, do wave
And whip the air — incorrigible kin — and beck'n
The ghostly shades and shadows that do haunt
The shaggy Shawangunks, and do point and nod
Their spectral bows menacingly at spooks,
That viewless roam the winds and shriek and moan

And make the des'late night a thousand fold
More dreary. Wheezingly the pine trees sigh
For Summer's wooing breath ; the road-side ice
Discharges ominous volleys at the cold,
And Nature in her grand but awful mood
Bewild'rs the weary trav'ler; dumbs his thoughts,
Who needs must see, and feel some mighty pow'r,
August, sublimely strange ; but dares not think —
The passive spell has froze the springs of thought.
Impression reigns, entrancing king, the while,
Till Reason roused from icy chills that calmed
Her powers, rends the 'numbing bonds and moulds
The chaos of the trav'ler's mind again
Into fair forms of thought.   He journeys on
A wild night-haunted road and thinks the thoughts
That few do dare to think when hemmed about
With threat'ning things they know not of, and in
A world far stranger yet, *to him,* than all
His thoughts may be to you ; so strange ! so strange !
But Fear's reaction on the mind gives thrice
The force to courage, and once the spooks of night
Dispersed, the heart grows brave, the soul more
        strong
To wage and win all other battles, be
They what they may, or long or short and fierce.

*   *   ⁎

A wall of stone now skirts the road along
Full many a weary pace.   He stops where some
Unusual width and height attracts and holds
Attention for a thought — to muse and dream :
Whence came these stones so chiseled round with
        wear ?
Whence came their atoms first of all and what
Hath loos'd them from the parent rock, and whence
The parent ? Whither art they bound ? Who knows!
What tale hath ev'ry sep'rate stone to tell
That rears this wall ? Ye dumb things speak ! not
        dumb,
More elequent than mortal tongue, they speak
A richer language : universal words
That have a meaning unmistakable, plain
And pure as truth to those who stood to learn
Their letters at the knee of nature ; those
Conversant with the wild-wood and the charms
Of tree for tree ; the fascination sweet
Among the flow'rs that bloom, all modest, rock'd
On sleepy zephyrs, sweetly soft, and sung
To rest with starry lulabies, and kissed
By am'rous Sol, and 'freshed by tears of his

Sad disappointed love, which lover-like
He 's oft renews as there be rays of Hope ;
And those who hear the voices of a tree
In leaf and bloom and listen with an ear
Of knowing sympathy to 'ts breath of sighs ;
And who commune with rocks and cloud-capp'd
     craggs,
And with instinctive short-hand take their notes
From brooks and birds, from cataracts and falls,
From tidal ebbs and flows, to such, each stone
Tells tales of thrilling tragedies and far
More history than's taught in schools and books.
Who built the wall, this old stone wall, so hoar
With frost and snow and fringed with mossy beard ?
The hands that placed it there have long ago
Been dust — the wall is holy !   Sacred shrine
Where Labor worship'd Love.   Upon it look
O, Stranger !   Seest thou not thereon it writ
In sacred stains of tears and manly sweat
The finger prints of Toil ; the blessed tale —
The loving romance of a hoping heart ?
And too, canst thou not hear that mingled strain —
A distant, happy song, divinely sweet,
And faint as ling'ring odors in a room
When one we love has gone — O poets' dream ! —

The children at their play! Ah, yes! Ah, me!
Too well these stones have kept each sight and
  sound,
Each shade and sun-kisst spot; and ev'ry phase
Of wild-wood life, and ev'ry throb and beat
Of nature lingers 'round them still and will
Yet linger longer in the future than
A human eye can see.

LOVE MUST HAVE HIS LOVE.

On nights like this when my blood runs riot
With the fever of youth and its mad desires.
                    ELLA WHEELER WILCOX.

Here in the gloaming, in this bower,
   Right here beneath the willow tree.
I met my love at this sweet hour
   And now I'm waiting here for thee,

My lusty mistress; do not wait
   For I am booked at eight to-night
To meet Fiance at her gate.
   O Time, O cease thy rapid flight!

Yet I am waiting! hang the clock,
   It's striking now the 'pointed hour!
Ah, here she comes!   I know the frock
   That glides beneath yon apple bower.

And now the storm of passion comes,
   And comes all clad in robes of light;
But ere the vortex reaches me
   The flame of love shall burn as white.

And now for Love's transporting sips!
 And now for dreamy flights above!
I lap the wine-dew from her lips,
 And quaff the nectar of her love.

I twine myself about her form
 As drift to drift of white snow flies;
We feel the rage of Passion's storm
 Which passes off in breath of sighs.

Nor deem it wrong! rebuke us not
 Ye children of an earth-born will;
For this is but our common lot,
 And love is love forever, still.

EBB TIDE.

From the dark of dying years
  Grows a face with violet eyes,
Tremulous through tender tears,—
  Warm lips heavy with rich sighs,—
Ah, they fade! it disappears,
  And with it my whole heart dies!

OWEN MEREDITH.

O take me back, thou rolling tide,
  Across thy ceaseless billows;
O, back again by Nellie's side;
  Beneath the weeping willows!

O, back again 'neath tree and star,
  Beneath the moon, or roaming
Where oft we sat with her guitar
  At even, after gloaming.

O, give me back the flowing spring,
  The katy-dids a-chirping;
The songs of love she used to sing,
  These idle songs usurping.

O, take me back to Nellie's arms
　　Upon her bosom resting ;
And let me feast upon her charms
　　No more this cold world breasting.

And fill her eyes with love again,
　　And set her heart to throbbing ;
Bring back the roses to her cheeks
　　E'en though the grave a-robbing.

O, take me back, thou fleeting years,
　　Restore my own lost treasure !
And dry away these burning tears
　　With breezes soft of pleasure.

　　　　＊　　＊　　＊

My love is dead and o'er her head
　　The dandelions blooming ;
My joy is dead and o'er its head
　　Regret's pale flow'rs are blooming.

INCONSTANCY.

We never feel the same emotion twice :
No two ships ever ploughed the selfsame billow.

ELLA WHEELER WILCOX.

I have it ! I declare :
The pulsing trill, the heart's
Impatient beat ; nerves a quiver —
My soul stuck full of darts :

    The eagerness,
    The blissfulness,
    The dreaminess,
    The hopefulness of love.

How I love her and adore her,
With what predilection woo her
With her fascinating amour,
O, how charming and engaging
Is my darling paramour.
More she loves me than I love her ;
Her's a constant, strong devotion,
Though she 's true as heaven above her
I am fickle as the ocean ;
For my love, unlike the compass,

Points with ev'ry changing notion :
Points and swerves with scented zephyrs,
Lingers after dreamy laces
And the curves of pink beneath. —
Charmed and thralled by pretty faces.
Am I sorry for her ever —
This dear, true love of mine —
As she longing, waits but for me
With a love that 's half divine ?

Yes ! I pity her and any woman,
  Who loving, yields to any man ;
For men at best oft lack the human
  And most belong to a lower clan.

SOLITUDE.

O, fair and sweet is the land o' dreams,
　And blissful are her mystic charms!
And happy they who wander there
　Or rest in Reverie's soothing arms.

'Tis there I woo calm Solitude —
　Dispassioned Goddess of the heart —
And there I walk and talk with her,
　And linger longest ere we part.

Fair Solitude's a winsome miss;
　Her charms are countless, pure and fair;
Her blessed smiles of sacred bliss
　She gives to me with transports rare.

She tells me tales and sings me songs,
　And coyly weaves my weft of dreams;
And rocks me on her peaceful breast
　Maternal like, enrobed in dreams.

And through their gauze of mystic lace,
　As a happy babe, half 'wake I lie,

And look up in her fairy face
   Content to live and there to die.

Her eyes — deep azure of the sky —
   With soulful love-light, beam above ;
While she with soft, entrancing touch
   Awakes my soul to leesome love.

With her I find more joyful life
   Than all the busy world can give ;
Nor would I trade for years of strife
   One blessèd hour with her to live.

For lover and mother to me is she ;
   And lover and mother will ever be,
As flame to moth and blossom to bee
   'Til the dead shall rise up from the sea, the sea.

THE GHOST OF THE MURDERED HEART.

A cold and snow-white corpse — a corpse
    All pale and cold and fair —
With streaming hair and eyes of fire,
And a look so wierd, yet filled with dire,
And a face not lined but sad with care
I've met in my wand'rings here and there
        In the dead of night.

And I thought I had dreamed a ghostly dream —
    A hideous, bold night-mare —
Forgot, in short, the eyes of fire,
Forgot the look — the glance so dire —
And thought no more of the face of care
I'd met in my wand'rings here and there
        In the pale moon-light,

'Til I sat one night, leagues deep in thought —
    In thought on things just read —
Soft footfalls — footfalls soft and low
As a dew drop falling off of a blow —

" Great God ! I shook, for I knew the tread :

Great God! I shook for I knew the tread;
Half turned in my chair and beheld the dead —
        The sad face white.

The lamp was burning; I was not asleep —
        If I was I am sleeping now —
My nerves were shocked to paralyze
As I gazed on the face, in the fiery eyes
Of the thing at my side I beheld, I vow!
As I saw it then, I see it now,
        Ere it took flight.

"O curse the thing or curse my sight"—
        I said to the spectre there —
"And curse those burning eyes of fire,
And curse thy look of hellish dire,
And curse thy sad, white face of care,
And curse thy raven, streaming hair
        Or leave my sight!"

As the Aspen trembles by soft winds blown —
        So trembled this ghost of the dead —
Then turning and fluttering as if to go.
It stopt for a moment, with accents slow,
Near the door, and spoke with the speech of the
    dead,
Then vanished away with a noiseless tread,
        As a thief from fright.

And these are the words it said,
Though said in the speech of the dead:
    "O, man of the world
    By passion hurled,
And led by a heartless flame;
    Beware of the coil
    That shall bind and shall foil
And devastate each claim,
    Each aim of thy life
    And keep thee in strife
    With thy heart!
If on murder bent
O, keep the sad rent
    Forever apart
    From the soul.
Go kill the woman
But if you are human
Don't murder her heart."

MID–MOST.

Love is not love, which alters when it alteration finds.

SHAKESPEARE.

Thy picture hangs upon the wall,
    Beside my bed, at this sweet hour,
When low the shades of twilight fall
    With soft, unconscious power.

The busy hum of Rosendale
    Has ceased, and falls like a weary bee ;
While over the Upenbacher's vale
    The twilight comes with thoughts of thee.

The whistle has spoken the hour of retreat,
When slowly, all homeward with sad, weary feet,
The rock-workers go—the coopers, and breakers of
    stone —
The men of grim brawn and of sinew and muscle and
    bone —
Gone from their labors to wife and repose,
Gone to their mothers, their sisters and sweethearts !
    who knows !

The boats have "laid to" at their moorings near by;
And the world seems at peace with itself and with
      men — save I —
I am hoping and aching and longing for thee.
(Art thou wishing and waiting and watching for me?)
I hear the piano all softly below
And hearing it many sweet thoughts of you grow
And blossom my heart with a rapturous glow
Of sweet memories.

  Thy picture there, those liquid eyes,
    These shadows here — entrancing gloom —
  Recall my vanished paradise
    From out the Past's lone tomb.

  Instinctively I turn to thee
    With thoughts of love, as flow'rs above
  To Sun ; as wind sighs, to a tree.
    And what does all this prove ?

  Thou art my sun; thy life the power
    That moulds this clay, that feeds this soul,
  That gives existence to this hour —
    This love — this glowing coal.

RONDOUT.

Dear old Rondout, how I love thee,
    Love thy water-lute and lay ;
Oft I held communion with thee
    On some drowsy summer day.

Oft upon thy bosom sporting,
    Have I dreamt my youthful dreams;
Often 'round thy shore cavorting
    Have I watched thy friendly gleams.

Thou hast been my friend and nearer
    Far than others of that name ;
Thou art now my friend and dearer ;
    How I love thy ancient name !

Flowing on to wed the Hudson,
    With thy winding, moody glide ;
Proudly will the grand old Hudson
    Swell his breast to meet his bride.

Dear old Rondout, I shall miss thee,
    Miss thy water-lute and lay ;
Dear old Rondout, I shall bear thee
    In my dreams though far away.

HOPE'S FALLING LEAVES.

Still young, I roam about the world
    And far from sweet content ;
My dreams of youth about me furl'd,
    On unknown journeys bent.

I wander here and wander there
    Like some drought stricken stream,
And search for flow'rs untouched with care : —
    My soul's ill-fated dream.

I search and seek ; I reach and wind,
    And long and hope in vain ;
With hungry heart and thirsting mind,
    My clouds bring me no rain.

I wander down some mountain side
    And in some valley see
My wish ; when there the hills divide
    My wisht-for nook from me.

To make my barren life more drear,
    And give my soul a keener sting ;
From bow'r and bush and sky I hear
    My leesome-lack, in bird-song ring.

" Avail thyself of youth and love ;
   Their fresh-born fulness and delight,
And soar in dreamy flight above
   Terrest'ral barrenness and night.

" Enjoy the May-bloom of thy life,
   And all the sweets of maiden flow'rs ;
For age is cold and spent with strife,
   And only *once* come youthful hours.

" Nor heed the sneer, the look of scorning ;
   Keep thy mind on freedom's feast
And bend thy gaze e'er on the morning,
   Nor mind the church, but 'ape' the priest.

"Go seek thy pleasures in their time,
And drink the sweetness of thy prime,
Thy bridge of youth, a span sublime,
     Of leesome rapture,
Inspiring all thy soul's hot race
For that enchanting, warm embrace
     We lose to capture,"

E'en thus, we gain : a lesson learned,
   Fresh coined, at Truth's own mint 'twas made —
One spark of knowledge sure discerned
   Is : with our joys comes always shade.

THOUGHTS OF A SUMMER DAY.

Diamonds are found in the dark places of the earth;
Truths are found only in the depth of thought.

VICTOR HUGO.

Who knows the human mind, and is conversant with

Those countless hosts, knows much ; this world hath
little else

To teach ; for mysteries only lie within the thoughts

Of men ; and thoughts tenfold mysterious are, and
deep

And wide as space. And God and Devil, Heav'n
and Hell

And Earth and Star, man and beast and ev'ry thing

There is or was, hath form and substance only in

The wide significance of universal thought.*

Both good and evil are but names compared with
place

And time, and have no universal measure stick

---

* It was long a troublesome question to my understanding whether or
not a fact could exist apart from the mental conception of it ; * * *
recognizing at the same time that every idea was produced directly or
indirectly by facts.

FROM AN UNPUBLISHED WORK.

Of truth, by which to gauge a fact ; two things alone
Preserve one universal standard weight, and they
Are Love and Hope — the only one immortal pair —
Eternal man and woman — parents of the soul
And sentiment — the god and goddess of the heart.
And he who worships them must be of lib'ral mind,
Must have both brain and heart and sympathies
    immense ;
In him there scarce can be a trace of bigot blood,
Nor hate, nor envy ; vengeance, vanity nor greed.
He needs must know that men who err are blind or
    weak
That life without a sinful act or falt'ring step
Exists but in angelic dreams ; that men at best,
See little and know less ; he pities those who fight
And hate like savage beasts o'er narrow, senseless
    creeds,
But bears no enmity toward them ; ·he sees in them
A childish ignorance, a longing after truth,
A wish to be aright, a struggle in the dark
Dim dungeon—Superstition—sees the priests grow
    fat
On inoffensive zeal put forth by those who fear
But reason not.   He knows : sublimest words e'er
    said

Are words least comprehended ; and that prejudices
Are simply mental robbers ; and that vices are
The vilest murderers ; that murdering hearts is worse
Than taking lives; and knows that "sacrifice of earth
To paradise is but to leave the substance for
The shadow."   He believes that men are like the
    plants :
None bad ; but by condition fated ill, and wild,
And grow untutored in neglected spots and waste
The soil through want.   He has no rigid form by
    which
To measure woman's virtue ; and sees in prostitution
The wretched yoke of heartless slavery — the gall —
The pain that weighs upon maternity, on grace
And feeble womanhood, on beauty and on charms.
Above all else, he knows that chisel how we may
This block of fate from which our lives are made,
    the streaks
And veins of destiny will never disappear.

" Stopt she 'neath a pine tree, trembling,
Where her father's warriors bled."

DEATH OF APUKWA.

A LEGEND OF WAWARSING.

Long ago, one quiet evening,
  As the Western purpling shades
Dropt their gauzy mantle over
  Napanoch's rough hills and glades,

Stole into that dreamy village,
  With a silent, stealthy tread,
Apukwa, Móhonk's only daughter ;
  Came she there to beg for bread.

For her father, aged and feeble,
  Dying in his birchen tent,
With the snows of age upon him —
  Winter-oak rough seamed and bent.

It was summer with dame Nature,
  And the air was fresh and sweet
With the wild flowers of the forest,
  And the balsam tall and steep.

Dreamy looked she at the landscape,
  In its darkening shadows veiled;
Deeply breathed she of the odors
  That the woods and flowers exhaled.

From the calm depth of her brown eyes
  Gleamed a gem in sadness set,
While some longing, loving, hoping
  Tear-drops made her eyelids wet.

Fate is voiceless, yet an instinct
  Oft presages her approach;
Ere she steps upon the threshold
  Oft her shadows there encroach.

Was there in this rich, red daughter,
  In her soul of fire and love,
Premonition of her danger?
  Scenes and glimpses from above!

Soon along the village gliding,
  Like a ghost or spirit fled,
Stopt she 'neath a pine-tree, trembling,
  Where her father's warriors bled.

And beneath the pine-tree trembling,
  By a white man she was spied; —

Mistaken for some lurking red man, —
    He shot her then, and there she died.

Ending thus a life, and leaving
    One she loved to die as well,
Illustrating Fantine, showing
    Fate to most of us is " hell."

WORD OF SYMPATHY

Ye boast of your learning and science,
  Ye sages of wisdom and lore ;
Ye boast of your generalization,
  Of " isms " you dig to the core ;
You tell us the beauties of nature
  As over the lenses you pore ;
You dig and you delve for the treasures
  All hid in a darksome, deep store ;
But of what avail are your labors
  While learning is pulseless and cold ;
Of what use are the beauties of nature
  Which lie hid beneath the drear wold ?

One ray of warm sunlight to gladden
  The eye of a flow'r or a man,
Is more in the plan of creation
  Than the whole of your learned-pate clan,

One word from a heart that is loving,
  When trouble is weighing us down,
Is more to a suffering person
  Than passionless wealth of a crown.

BABES.

I like to hear children at the table telling what big things they have seen during the day. I like to hear their merry voices mingling with the clatter of knives and forks. I had rather hear that than any opera that was ever put upon the stage.

R. G. INGERSOLL.

Whose heart is alien to the love of babes
And feels no kinship with their simple ways,
Nor feels the blitheness of their budding days
Must be a wretch indeed, devoid of heart.
For what can take the place of children's love,
Their glad, unburdened souls, so light and free,
That play upon our hearts a melody
As sweet and warm and pure as heav'n above ?
God bless the children ! bless their fleeting days
With gladness and the innocence of truth ! —
Fair bursting buds of morn, that ope in bloom
Of richest fancy, dreams and hopeful lays,
And rosy hues that fill the air of youth —
Too soon dispersed by frosts that veil the tomb.

ODE TO NATURE.

Lo ! where the apple blossoms bloom
   And wingèd songsters sport and play,
Fair Nature sat beside her loom,
   And wove her flow'ry lay.
The dandelions' disks of gold,
Besprinkled o'er the meadow-wold
   With butter-cups and daisies gay —
The notes on Nature's music sheet
All set to pleasure soft and sweet,
   She sang throughout the day.

And there amid the flow'rs of spring,
   In dreamy vales I ween,
She wanders there her songs to sing
   Composed upon the green.
And there beside some rippling brink,
She stops with Solitude to think —
   Calm Solitude, her cous'n, mayhap —
Upon the songs she ne'er has sung
Since th' proud old Earth was 'n infant young,
   And cradled in her lap.

And what's the organ of her touch
  So delicately strung ? —
The varied strains our heart chords touch
  With music ever young.
It is the breath of forest trees,
The streams and seas and birds and bees ;
  Rich harmony she flings
Upon the billowy atmosphere
Pervading space both far and near,
  Ah, this is the song she sings.

BONNIE BROOKLYN MARY.

In the passion and pain of her kisses
Life blooms to its richest and best.
ELLA WHEELER WILCOX.

I have a passion for the name of " Mary."
BYRON.

It's my bonnie Brooklyn Mary,
    Soft of eye and pure, deep-hearted ;
It's my darling, sweet-heart Mary
    That I dream of since we parted.

Ne'er was there a woman purer
    With her tropic, purling passion ;
Ne'er was there more sweet allurer
    Of my soul's full throbbing passion.

Oft do I recall her poses
    And her blue veined fairy billows ;
Dreaming, feast upon her roses ;
    Sleeping on her breasts for pillows.

For my love won her devotions
    And our hearts beat for each other,

And our souls are *one*, though oceans
   Roll between the one and other.

All descriptions of her fail me ;
   Who can paint with words a woman ?
E'en conceptions nearly fail me
   Of this ideal, lovely woman.

Yet I know her form is perfect
   Sculptured out by Artist Nature ;
And the wealth of all creation
   Help compose her faultless stature.

And my love for her is worship,
   While my joy with her is heaven ;
Nor have known a purer worship
   Nor would wish a sweeter heaven.

For her mind is like her person,
   Pure and true, a perfect union ;
And her soul blooms forth in fragrance
   Of divinity in woman.

So my bonnie Brooklyn Mary,
   Soft of eye and pure, deep-hearted ;
It's of you, my sweet-heart Mary
   That I dream of since we parted.

WINTER ROSES.

O, lady fair, the biting air
  Too roughly smites thy cheek;
O, lady fair, the frosty air
  Brings roses to thy cheek;
O, let me pluck them with a kiss
  None wilt thou lose thereby;
The more I pluck, the less you'll miss!
  Come, quick, love, lest they fly!

O, lady-love, the stars above
  Look down with calm delight;
O, lady-love, the sky above
  So beautiful to-night,
Cannot compare wi' your rich black hair:
  The stars wi' your eyes so bright.
Come love! may I pluck the roses there?
  She nods with a smiling air.

Nor should you love, when stars above
  Look down a shimmer sheen.

My lady-love, the stars above
　　Ne'er tell what they have seen ;
Beneath their gaze, a misty haze
　　Envelopes many a fair
And rosy maid, who loving laid
　　Where joy dispells all care.

THE OLD SONGS.

O thou companion of my youth !
    My childhood's playmate, fond and true,
O sing the old songs once again
    While I, sweet love, draw near to you.

Yes, sing the old songs once again
    And touch the organ soft and low;
While I in dreamy ecstasy
    Recall the days o' the " Long ago :"

The dear lost days we used to see —
    The happy days of childhood fair,
When all the world was bright to me,
    And joyous life ne'er knew a care.

When " Island* " flow'rs more fair and sweet
    Than any growing there to-day,
I plucked and lay them at your feet
    Or wreathed your brow in happy play.

The play-house 'neath the locust tree
    A palace rich I thought it then,

*A well watered piece of woods in Ulster.

With broken dishes scattered free ;
   And rich to us it was I ken.

For wealth lies in the human mind,
   Whether wealth in gold or wealth in heart ;
And growing old we're sure to find
   Our richest joys the first to part.

The little cart we used to ride,
   The boat, the dolls and all are gone,
With naught but memory now to hide
   The wrecks of days that long have flown.

Then sing the old songs once again,
   And touch the organ soft and low ;
While I through mellow dreams of pain
   Recall the days o' the long ago.

Now let me take thee in my arms,
   And let me feel thy throbbing heart,
Recalling all our childhood's charms
   And joys I pray may never part.

O, thou companion of my youth,
   My childhood's playmate fond and true !
Come, breath the old songs once again
   While I, sweet love, draw near to you.

A SONNET TO COL. ROBERT G. INGERSOLL.

"Our" Ingersoll! O child of happy fate ɪ
Thou art well crowned with laurels fair and true,
For millions bring their tributes unto you
All fresh and warm, from hearts humanely great.
Thy grand position in the world of thought
And common sense is quite unique ; but *one*
Thou art in this great world, yet like the sun
Thou givest light and heart all richly wrought
In warp and woof of Love and Hope to all
Our race.   Thy classic verse, of beauty rare,
Alive with throb and beat of joy and truth,
And bright with sparkling gems of wit, shall fall
Not vainly down the ages, full and fair,
But thrill their heart with everlasting youth.

UNTOLD.

I worked all day in an ice-house,
　　Storing the blocks away,
And talked with their voiceless crystals,
　　That I sought to keep from decay.

I asked them of their journey,
　　Of·a thousand things that day ;
And they drew me pictures from mem'ry
　　As I placed the blocks away.

And they told me many a story,
　　And legends quaint and old ;
But the rarest things they told me
　　Will never be retold.

IN LOVE'S TANGLED WEB OF DREAMS.*

She touches my cheek and I quiver —
I tremble with exquisite pains.

ELLA WHEELER WILCOX.

What can I do and how can I be
Any thing else but a servant of thee?
Thou with thy face so radiant and rare,
Framed in soft tresses of chestnut-brown hair;
Thou with thy loving looks tender and true —
O queen of my heart! what else can I do?

What can I do and how can I be
Any thing else but true unto thee?
Thou with thy charms, surpassing, supreme;
Thou with thy figure — a poet's dream —
Thou with thy loving-heart constant and true —
O queen of my life! what else can I do?

What can I do and how can I be
Any thing else but thy slave-devotee?

---

* To a fair, sweet daughter of Ulster.

Thou with thy wealth of beauty and grace,
Thou with thy Raphael-Madonna-face,
Thou with thy roses of tenderest hue
O dream of my soul! what else can I do?

What can I do and how can I be
Any thing else but a lover of thee?
Thou who art pure as Love's own self,
Thou its creator and thou its elf,
Thou passion — the sweetest that mortal can woo,
O light of my life! what else can I do?

What can I do and how can I be
Any thing else but a dreamer of thee?
Thou who art perfect, the sweetest on earth,
Thou Angel of Joy, disperser of dearth,
Thou gem of the morning, sweet spirit of dew,
O blood of my heart, what else can I do?

What can I do and how can I be
Any thing else but a drop in the sea —
A drop in the sea of thy shoreless love —
A drop — then a mist in strata above,
Warmed into mist by your glowing love free,
O Sun of my heaven! what else can I be?

What can I do and how can I be
Any thing else but a singer of thee ?
Thou the sole star of my ev'ry night,
Thou chaser away of my ev'ry blight ;
My beautiful bride the seasons through,
O wife of my SOUL ! what else can I do ?

What can I do and how can I be
Any thing else but devoted to thee ?
Thou maker of happiness, pleasure and bliss,
Charming my soul away with thy first kiss,
Melting my life thou hast mingled us two —
O wife of my HEART ! WHAT ELSE COULD WE DO ?

ASTROLOGY.

Of all the songs that poets sing
   The best to me by far,
Are those which to my senses bring
   The myst'ries of a star.

O, stars of love and stars of hope
   That through the distance peer,
And cheer us onward as we grope
   Through ages dark, and drear.

We know your magic —feel the spell
   That moulds us to our fate ;
O, stars of heaven and stars of hell !
   O, stars that never wait.

O, swinging censers of the night !
   O, flow'rs of heaven's blue !
O, symbols of some boundless might !
   O, petals of blended hue.

FLAKES OF SNOW.

All silently the snow-flakes fall and lay
Their mantle — fair symbolic peace — as pure
As heaven o'er the earth.   Mysterious robe
Of shadow! Cold and colorless, both old
And new and shapeless as the wind, yet real
As truth and strange as life and fair as flow'rs —
A flow'r itself of other flow'rs inwove ;
What art thou? Cometh whence, and whith'r away?
Thou spectral thing! Thou jeweled ghost that haunts
The moonlight and the starlight—ghost of tears !
Tell some of thy rich history ! Art thou dumb?
Replies a voice from mystic depths of air —
That strange and fickle wilderness that hems
Us in and makes us slaves to 'ts changing mood,
And loosens its fierce denizens of cold
And heat upon us, forcing us to find
A shelter from their furies, lest we die
A prey to their insatiate, heartless greed,
" Yes ! dumb to those with sightless eyes and ears
Too blunt to hear; to mindless, thoughtless men —
Devoid of soul, of empty heart and those

Whose nerves have never felt a thrill, a throb,
A beat of pain, of pleasure ; I converse
With poets and my language is a song
That's writ on air — a mingled song of mirth
And pathos — tales of tragedy and joy,
And such as never yet were writ by man
Nor penn'd upon the tablet of his mind —
(Ah ! small it is at best to write upon —)
And ev'ry sep'rate snow-flake here has more
To tell than all man's mental leaves can hold.
Far more than human souls can comprehend.
For ev'ry snow-flake is a page, a book,
Of wondrous, endless history ; and speaks
Of things innumerable : Nature's lore and all
Her legends of exhaustless length, and themes
So strange to man, so foreign to his ken
And custom that to speak their names would be
As meaningless as "Time," "Eternity,"
Or "Magnitude" — perforce all empty names ;
Look ! Look ! yon snow-flake, larger than the rest
About it, see it fall all sullenly
To earth and heavy-hearted, disappear
In one vast sheen of down ? Why so ? you ask !
Because yet scarce a year ago it fell
Upon the happy breast of a fair bride —

A heaving, love-beat breast that warm'd the heart
And thrill'd the soul and cheered the life of him,
Her chosen lord as they rode out one day.
And there it lay and list unto her voice
Of music, sweetly clear and pure and true —
A happy poem of love — and heard replies
From his great, manly heart ; and heard their plans
Laid out in hopeful bliss, and joined them in
One long sweet ecstasy — a kiss ; a kiss :
Most sacred thing on earth — at home as well
In sorrow as in joy ; and there it lay
And heard the lore of love — O, priceless thing ! —
Restruck in hearty, happy chime, and e'en
The drossless gold, recast again as oft
Before into the magic moulds of words.
It lay upon her breast until her breath
Of holy love dissolved it to a dream
Of mist ; it went its way through paths of air
Ne'er trod by mortal man, until one day
In early Autumn, when September's tears
Were falling and the sky seemed veiled with pain,
It fell upon a coffin's glass exposed
Beside an open grave, for one last look —
A ling'ring, loving look — of husband at
His wife who claspt upon her silent breast

A tender babe.   This wife, who but a bride
Of yesterday, and on whose breast this flake
Of snow did rest so brief a time ago,
Lies cold and dead there now, and on her bier
A tear was shed — a tremulous tear of woe ;
Nor came it from a human eye, but from
The stricken air — a melted flake of snow."

LIFE AND LOVE IN THE SHAWANGUNKS.

"O happy love ! where love like this is found."

It is better to be the emperor of one loving and tender heart, and she the empress of yours, than to be the emperor of the world.

R. G. INGERSOLL.

When white the robe of winter fell
    Upon the Shawangunk's breast,
And drear the valley landscape lay,
    Meandering from the west
One Sunday morn, I journeyed 'long
    The Shawangunk's northern wing
To where a woodman's cabin stood
    Beside a mountain spring.

Paul Langè was the woodman's name,
    A man of noble birth,
A scholar and a gentleman,
    A man of sterling worth :
He left his home in Germany
    Full thirty years ago
To build a home, seek quiet life,
    Nor caring he for show.

" * * * * a woodman's cabin stood
Beside a mountain spring."

And here among the Shawangunks blue
    He met and loved his wife :
A dark-eyed, winsome woman, true,
    A jewel in his life.
And here among the mountains wild
    He built his humble home,
And dwelleth here with wife and child,
    Nor careth he to roam.

And often round his roaring hearth
    When winter's chilling blast
Was howling 'round his cottage eaves
    He'd oft recall the past :
And tell me tales of college days :
    Adventure 'cross the sea ;
He'd tell me tales and sing me songs,
    As often thrilling me.

And oft we'd fill our wooden pipes
    And oft our empty glass ;
Discussing *this*, reviewing *that*,
    The night would quickly pass ;
For there beneath his humble roof
    The purest pleasures dwell ;
And there beside his hearty board
    My hunger oft I'd quell.

And of the woodman's lonely life
    I'd often question him :
"And why forsake the busy world
    And grow thy learning dim
My friend ?" quoth I one ev'ning drear
    When th' wind was choked with snow,
And struggling through the leafless trees
    Ferociously did blow.

"My friend," said he, "the woodman's life
    Is not a lonely one !
What need have I for other life
    Beneath the stars or sun ?
I'm living here in Nature's heart
    And my heart beats content
'Mid all the charms that man can have
    Upon this continent.

"Nor lonely am I here I trow,
    With birds, and brooks, and air
To breath, quite free from city filth ;
    And endless flowers fair,
For 'tis not solitude to be
    With nature, heart to heart ;
My books of trees and stones and streams
    For Greek I would not part.

"And mark you well, my boy," said he,
　"The home of solitude
Is not with nature, nor with me :
　The city 's its abode, —
That wilderness — humanity —
　Where glitters tinsel gold,
And greed and lust and direful need
　Make virtue bought and sold."

A LOCK OF HAIR.

" One stream of her soft hair strayed unconfined
Down her ripe cheek, and shadowed her deep eyes.'

Small curl of nut-brown hair — a dream
Of loving transport.   Ah, the seam,
Or thread of gold that links the past
To me·! thou bonnie gem ! thou stream
     Of Nellie's hair !—
Sweet fragment of the past : sole gleam
Athwart my sombre life of care
     That gives me hope.

My mem'ry's darling ! sweetest thought,
That fills my soul, of rapture wrought,
Is this blue-ribboned curling lock
I took from Nellie's brow, nor sought
     A greater bliss.
She gave it me one Autumn, frought
With mellow sun-light and the kiss
     Of ripened fruit.

Ah, well do I remember them : words
Of love, from rosy lips, that birds ·

At mating time might imitate,
So full of music and of love
        Divinely great.
And looks !—the inward light, that floods
The sensual world and makes it pure ;
        I feel again

The sacred spell, the very trills
That floated through me, all the thrills
That shook my soul and made my life
One blessed span of ecstasy,
        So fair and free,
As on that autumn morn, with face
Upturned and radiant with grace,
        And beautiful,

She gave me vows, a lock of hair,
A locket cased her picture fair,
She gave me *all*, to enhance my bliss
Her melting form, threw in a kiss
        And parted we.
But time has flown and left a thorn
Within my hope of her who born
        My infant boy.

MAN.

Wind of Winter, sun of Summer,
    Breezy breath of Autumn,
Green of Spring and all the glimmers
    Of the dew ;
Robe of Winter, tears of Summer
    Blended hues and shimmers,
    This is man.
*A man's life is a strange life
And the ways of men are strange, strange ways.

Rush of rivers, calm of waters,
    Murmuring brooks of meadows,
Songs of birds and all the voices
    Of the wood ;
Blue of heaven, pale of star-light,
    All the works of nature,
    This is man.
A man's life is a strange life
And the ways of men are strange, strange ways.

---

* After Longfellow.

Heaven's mercy, angels' goodness,
    Hellishness and hating,
Loving kindness, — glowing manhood
    Of the heart.—
Passion's hunger, wild beasts' plunder,
    Untamed furies brutal ;
    This is man.
A man's life is a strange life
And the ways of men are strange, strange
    ways.

BENEATH THE GOLDEN-ROD.

Who makes my bed at night
   And turns down the cover ?
Who keeps the sheets and pillows white ?
   My mother ! O, my mother.

Who sings her babes to rest,
   And tucks in the cover ?
Who kisses each and calls them " blessed ?"
   My mother ! O, my mother.

Who sings us songs at eve
   As night drops her cover !
Who tells us tales which we believe ?
   My mother ! O, my mother.

Who takes us out to walk —
   " Me and little brother ?"
Who listens to our childish talk ?
   My mother ! O, my mother.

Who teaches us to pray —
   " Me and little brother ?"

Who tells us what in prayer to say?
  My mother, O, my mother.

*   *   *

Long years have fled, my heart has bled
  From many an aching tear;
My heart has bled, my joy has fled
  Before dark clouds of care.

*   *   *

Who lies beneath the sod—
  Beneath the grave's green cover?
Who sleeps beneath the golden-rod?
  My mother, O, my mother.

Who travels there to mourn,
  With tears damp her cover?
Who, weary, old, of joy all shorn?
  "Me and little brother."

SHIPWRECKED.

I stand on the shore of the Restless,
  On a beach of shifting sands;
And I cry to the desert relentless
  That beckons with fated hands :

" O, give me back my child-hood,
  Its days of summer weather,
The perfume of the wild-wood,
  The flowers I used to gather."

I call to receding billows,
  That from me far have flown,
To come as downy pillows,
  Renewing the dreams I've known.

I signal my barks o' fancy,
  That sailed from the port of Youth,
And skimming the distance smoothly,
  Forsake me, alas! for sooth!

I wail to wilds around me ;
  I call aloud and moan ;

I reach for things beyond me
  And strive and struggle and groan.

I cry aloud and listen,
  The answer comes — an echo —
I turn where Hope's stars glisten
  And toward the dawn turn also ;

Yet like a ship-wrecked sailor,
  On unknown, rock-bound coasts,
Cast from some hapless whaler
  I live in a land of ghosts.

I cry to the Past all vainly,
  I search, but do not find ;
I peer in The Future dimly,
  I ask — replies the wind.

How long on the shore of the Restless,
  On this beach of shifting sands,
Must I cry to the desert relentless
  That beckons with fated hands.

" O, give me back my childhood,
  Its days of summer weather,
The perfume of the wild-wood,
  The flowers I used to gather.

" O give me back my lost days, —
  My guileless, blessèd treasures —
O, give me back the sweet ways
  To my childhood's sylvan pleasures !

" O, take me on thy bosom
  And roll thy billows back,
Thou restless, eternal ocean !
  To childhood take me back.

"I am so tired and weary,
  And my soul is hungry too,
A-roaming these cold sands dreary,
  O take me back to you !

"Take me 'eternal ocean,'
  Great mother of us all,
And mantle my heart in your bosom,
  Your tresses let be my pall ! "

I gaze through the mists and the sadness,
  That befog these shifting sands,
Afar out on the hazy Relentless
  That beckons with fated hands.

And beckons and points to the eastward,
  To the dawn delayed but sure,

Where the hopes of our hearts may go forward
And cancérous hearts find cure.

I counsel thee ; trust in the future,
Ye with loads of wretched pain,
For the dawn of the day is before thee,
And sunshine follows rain.

The past is gone, nor recall it,
Like a dream it fades away,
And bears on its bosom 'long with it
The night as well as the day.

TO CHARLES STEWART PARNELL.

Dec. 24, 1890.

Parnell ! O, leader of the Irish cause !
Protector of a nation, patriot pure·
And helmsman brave, pursue thy course nor pause
In thy endeavor for the ease and cure
Of Irish wrongs.   Art thou not lov'd, ador'd ?
A million hearts beat quicker at the sound
Thy name inspires.   Heed not the vulgar horde
Of thy pursuers.   Thou 'rt above a wound
Of falsehood.   Slander ne'er can mar nor blot
Thy spotless record, sacred to the heart
Of ev'ry free man, Irishman or not.
Thy guiding hand cannot be spared apart
From its design.   And millions look at you
In admiration, as at some giant rock
Storm hem'd, wave beat, serene ; and on the blue
Unrest we hail thee, proud above the shock —
Unconq'rable hero ! Ireland's truest friend.

THE STORM.

I sit at my window watching
  A storm that beats the pane :
In angry fury dashing
  The tear drops of the rain.

And sitting here I ponder,
  A-watching the falling tears,
And watching them I wander
  Through a labyrinth of years.

Through pre-historic ages
  I tread the desert — Past —
And in its fossil pages
  My thoughts in moulds are cast.

Until through mists and mazes,
  And checkered sun and shade,
I see through changing hazes,
  The progress life has made.

For ev'ry rain-drop falling
  I know some heart has bled ;
For ev'ry wind-voice calling
  I know some soul has fled.

For ev'ry rain-drop falling
   Some mighty page is writ,
Of hist'ry sweet or galling.
   E'en 's a-musing, here I sit,

In ev'ry rain-drop falling
   The weft of legends old,
Echos each wind-voice calling
   From craggy peak and wold.

And many a vagrant fancy
   Came singing through my brain
As I sat at my window watching
   The tear-drops on the pane.

I sat at my window watching
   A storm that beat the pane,
In angry fury dashing
   The tear-drops of the rain.

And sitting there I pondered,
   A-watching the falling tears,
And watching them I wandered
   Through a labriynth of years.

A LOVER'S PLEA.

The wintry winds are moaning, Minna dear,
And the leafless trees are groaning, Minna dear,
    And the feath'ry pines are sighing
    And the seasons, they are dying
    And my heart to thee is flying
    All for true love, Minna dear ;
    Darling Minna ! Minna dear.

My heart for love is aching, Minna dear,
Which but *thou* canst keep from breaking, Minna
      dear,
    And my soul for thee is yearning,
    And my love for thee is burning,
    And all other love is spurning,
    All for thy love, Minna dear,
    Darling Minna, Minna dear.

But Summer's breath will woo thee, Minna dear,
And fair Summer's bloom will kiss thee, Minna
      dear,

And will flush thy cheeks to glowing,
And will rush thy love to flowing,
And will start thy blood to going
Ever faster, Minna dear,
Lovely Minna, Minna dear.

And the wild flow'rs they will cheer thee, Minna
          dear,
And the song-birds will not fear thee, Minna dear,
And the Muse will wake thee, thrilling,
And will set thy heart-chords trilling,
And thy *husbands'* heart fulfilling,
All with true-love, Minna dear,
Darling Minna, Minna dear.

But thy lover, heavy hearted, Minna dear,
From his idol must be parted, Minna dear,
And though from thee, of thee dreaming,
Till his life of thine be seeming,
And his soul, surcharged, be teeming,
All with true-love, Minna dear,
Lovely Minna, Minna dear.

Wilt thou think of me, O, sweet one, Minna dear,
When the gulf of time divides us, many a year?

Wilt thou think of me in kindness,
For I love you, dear, to blindness?
Wilt thou think of me in sadness,
For I love you, dear, to madness—
Of thy *true-love*, Minna dear,
Darling Minna, Minna dear?

If thou wilt then as a token, Minna dear,
Let thy vow at once be spoken, Minna dear,
    And draw near me in my sadness,
    Kiss me once just for my madness,
    Once, O, love, just for my blindness!
    Kiss me, think of me in kindness
    O, my darling, Minna dear,
    Lovely Minna l Minna dear.

ISLANDS.

O, vex me not with thinking
On the days that come no more,
Of the Islands in the river,
Of the ripples on the shore.
Of the days and weeks of sunshine
And the hours of holy pleasure,
Made by mem'ry ever brighter,
Ever sweeter, ever better,
As the tides of time roll on.

Teach us to forget, O Fate,
O, stern and awful ruler,
The joys, the songs and laughter,
The music's tender mirth
The sun that gilded bygone
Paths; the happy flow'rs I plucked;
Go hide them, dark Forgetfulness:
Our treasures, one and all,
And bury them deep and lone !
Only hush, sad voice of sighs,
And scatter, O, clouds of pain.

OLD ELI.

Upon a summer afternoon,
   One breezy, dusty day,
I chanced to meet upon the road
   A man quite old and gray,
Who held within his stiff'ning arm
   A child of tender years ;
And dust was on the infant's face,
   Its eyes bedimmed with tears.

The old man stopt for I knew him well
   And I shook his horny hand ;
We talked of rain and common things
   While he held on my hand,
For though a sinful man was he
   To all the church folks 'round
I liked him for I knew him well
   And knew his heart was sound

In spite of all his moral ills,
   The peculiar life he led ;
He'd oft get drunk and curse and swear,
   And seek a lustful bed,

And fight and quarrel when " run " upon,
　　And make a hideous din ;
For all his sense of moral law
　　Forsook him in his gin.

His face was rough with shaggy beard,
　　His eyes were gray as steel,
His form was bent which once was straight
　　His gait was half a reel ;
And yet withall a kinder heart,
　　I ween, ne'er beat a breast
Beneath his rough exterior,
　　A warm heart beat and prest.

" Barnhart," said I, " what have you there ?
　　Whose babe is that ? " I said.
He drew the infant close to him,
　　I saw, at heart he bled,
" Why this is mine ! " with mirthful feign,
　　" Whose would it be ! " said he,
" I love the child and he loves me,
　　That's why its mine, you see !

The mother of this youngen here—
　　Poor ailin', sickly boy,

Is young an' poor, forsook is she
  An' can't support the boy,
So, ez they put him on the town,
  I thought I'd bring him up,
And care for him the best I could,
  An' try to help him up.

I raised my boys by Sal an' Kate
  An' raised them youngens o' Janes'
An' raised 'em all the best I could
  An' took the best o' pains
To keep 'em shod an' fed an' clothed,
  Nor ever whipped 'em once ;
For whippin' aint no good to boys;
  It's sure to make 'em a dunce.

An' how d'er 'spose that I could see
  This child 'mong strangers go,
When 'ts mother's keepin' house for me,
  An' I'm abl' to hoe ?
An' Betsy, when she sees her boy
  Agin, an' hugs him tight,
My old heart will grow young agin
  At sich a loving sight.

An' bring me back my other days,
    An' sights that I haint see
Fer many a lame, ole grumblin' year,
    An' a child fer on my knee,
I aint no church man, much, "said he,
    Fer of Hell I haint no fear,
But fer dumb brutes an' babes "said he,
    You 'll allus find me here."

FORBIDDEN FRUIT.

" You might as well forbid the sea for to obey the moon.'
                                    SHAKESPEARE.

My Josie and I
  Were lovers for years,
We met and were wed
  'Neath a host of fears,
In secret we met
  In secret were wed ;
Our marriage was heaven,
  And bliss was our bed.

My Josie is fair
  As the flow'rs of May,
Roses bloom sweetly
  On her cheeks to-day ;
Her sensitive mouth,
  In passionate curves,
Bewitches me quite ;
  Reduces my nerves.

But what can we do,
  She's another's wife,
This queen of my heart,
  This gem of my life ;
Ah, strange this may seem
  To those who know not
The transports of joy
  In danger of shot. .

But such is the case
  And rightful or no,
A law without heart
  Says " reap as you sow ;"
So reaping I sow ;
  And sowing I reap
The pleasures of life
  From a dangerous steep.

And loyal to nature
  And true to my self
I journey cross lots
  To woo the young elf
That man has called Love ;
  And like all the streams

I wander me down
  Rich valleys and seams.

And unto my fold
  I gather them in :
Fountains of pleasure
  Nor deem it a sin ;
Nor shape I the course
  As onward I flow
Through landscapes of Fate,
  But reap as I go.

A POET'S LIFE.

" A life misunderstood is sad as tears."

The currents of a poet's life
    Are seldom understood ;
They ebb and flow content above
    The strata : care and strife
When 'circled in the arms of love.

THE OLD, OLD STORY.

'Twas not, I say, in ancient day,
 Nor yet of recent date,
A peasant boy, bare-foot, at play
 Swung 'round on the barn-yard gate.

The air was fine, the sun did shine
 Upon late flow'rs of spring;
The orchard white, like sea of brine
 Did foam with bloom of spring.

The sky was blue in dreamy hue,
 Drap'd 'round with fleecy white;
The breezes few that gently blew
 Brought odors of delight.

The songs of bird, the sweetest heard ·
 Flowed softly through the boughs;
The bleat of sheep among the herd
 Of grazing swine and cows,

The only sound that did resound
 In discord rude and dry;

On robes of green, in gold-spun sheen
   The Sunday's sun shone high,

When past the peasant's farm-house door,
   A stately carriage drove,
That held a lady and her lord
   On way to mountain grove.

They passed the door, but at the bore
   Of 'n ancient well they stopped ;
He stopped to drink but she the more
   To glance at peasant life.

Then beckoned she unto the boy
   A-leaning on the gate,
And plied with many questions coy
   His dreams of future fate.

Surprised at his high views of life
   She thought the more and more
Upon the cares and dreary strife
   The peasants must endure.

"And yet," she thought, "how happy seems
   This dreamy peasant boy,
Who bathed in light of Hopes' fair beams
   His future 's only **joy**."

Thus long she mused and oft she thought
   She saw his sunny face
Till through her dreams bright threads were wrought
   Of gold that she could trace

Throughout the web of her busy life
   Back to a barnyard gate ;
But years less full of joy than strife
   Did work to weave her fate.

And years did roll and time did toll
   The bell of warning note
Till gradually its accents dole
   Did drown this feeble mote
       Of memory.

As tide flowed on this peasant lad
   In nature's school was taught ;
And mingling with her num'rous glad
   And radiant forms, he fought

The awful battle — desert youth
   Where Poverty is king —
His bible, earth and flow'rs ; and truth
   He made his mental king.

Thus schooled, thus taught, he fought his way
  To manhood's honest sphere,
At manhood's dawn one autumn day
  He met this lady dear
        By accident.

        *   *   *

To tell the rest would be to tell
  The old, old story over ;
The tale of how a woman fell
  Prey to a youthful lover.

MIST AND CHANGE.

The mind is like a river,
　　Its 'fed from many a source ;
It wanders just like water
　　And changes oft its course.

At early dawn it voices
　　The brooklets' song in mountains,
And lovingly rejoices
　　In sunny mists of fountains.

It gurgles, sighs, and moaning
　　It chafes the stubborn shore ;
It whispers, asks with groaning
　　For days that come no more.

It pencils on its surface
　　In lines and ripples plain,
The hidden things within it :
　　The bars and snags of pain.

Just só, the lines and laughter
　　On human faces show

The reefs and rocks of danger —
   The hidden things below.

It rushes on and rages,
   And surges over rocks;
It roars o'er shallow places
   But through Time's hoary locks

Is sifted from its spirit,
   Its feeble race is run
Into the ocean near it,
   That bears them one by one

Within her proud old bosom,
   A-heaving to the sun;
And gives back crystal treasure
   Which airy journeys cover,
And gush in springs of pleasure
   And live the old lives over.

So each thing changes ever
   Along its winding course,
Throughout life's misty river
   From the ocean to its source.

A NIGHT IN THE SHAWANGUNKS.

When wild mid-winter's 'numbing blast
   Fills all the air with snowing,
And wierd the Shawangunk's howling crags
   Resent the wind's mad blowing,

I left the low-land village town,
   With many hearth-stones glowing,
My Shawangunk staff within my hand,
   My fingers often blowing.

The night was dark and from the north
   The freezing storm was raging,
And harpy whispers in the air
   More spritely things presaging.

I battled hard to keep the path
   Which through the woods went trailing,
While through the pines and rocky vales
   The ghostly storm was wailing.

At length I reached a craggy ledge
   When north to westward looking,
I saw the light from Langè's cot,
   His wife, late supper cooking.

Then struggled on to reach his door,
    Which opes when I but tap it,
And for his hearty, homely fare,
    Ah, freely does he share it.

The door I reach with welcome true,
    Then at his table, steaming,
We sit us down and eat and drink
    With kindly mirth all beaming.

While near to us with cleanly mien,
    His wife, the table serving,
Joins in our jokes, with hearty laugh,
    At strokes of wit sent verving.

And then with pipe and ruby flask
    Beside his wood-fire burning,
We sit and talk and drink and smoke,
    All wintry weather spurning.

Nor happier times have known than those
    When Shawangunk's snows were falling
And visiting my faithful friend,
    Sweet mem'ries oft recalling.

TO MRS. GEN'L CUSTER.

O, if there is a theme more worthy
  A sacred poet's song
Than virtuous maidenhood or woman,
  Then class me with the wrong.

O, tender, loving, constant woman !
  O, sweet-heart good and true !
The highest niche this side of heaven, —
  The trait I bless in you.

JEALOUSY.

The Morn was melting up the east,
   The West was gray as steel,
While Love partaking of his feast
   No sense of shame could feel;

For Magnet Love had found his Love
   And Passion's heat was white,
While disappearing stars above
   Shrank 'way from *such* a sight.

The old-maid Moon was pale with shame;
   The Sun rose blushing red,
While bursting throbs from Passion's flame
   Was raging o'er Love's bed.

The Sun in anger smote the Sky,
   The Sky returned the blow;
And thus up in the heavenly high
   They each struck blow for blow.

And there above the misty clouds
  The battle fierce increased,
Until the Night with stately tread
  Walked up the concave east.

"And what is all this time about?"
  Up spoke the Evening Star;
"'Twas all because of jealousy!"
  Came echoing from afar.

HOME.

The home where virtue dwells with love is like a lily with a heart of fire—the fairest flower in all the world.
R. G. INGERSOLL.

O, Home! thou magic, soothing name!
Thou synonym for love's true flame,
O, hallowed thought! From hope 'twas born
Possessing which it laughs to scorn
All other concepts of the mind
However true and well defined;
O, home! O presence pure and calm!
Sweet soulful air: the hearts' best balm;
O sacred spot! O heav'nly blend
Of love and hope; nor time can rend,
Thee from the blessed name of *friend.*

THE BELL OF THE BROKEN HEART.

"There are some things quite hard to understand."
The engineer stood in his cab, his heart,
Beat quick and strong ; the time drew near to start
His train ; he grasped the bell-rope in his hand,
When past him rolled a bridal party gay ;
He saw the bride and saw that she was fair ;
Then looked again and saw her auburn hair ;
That was enough ! he saw no more that day
Nor e'er again ; his Love to him was lost ;
Death's pallor spread his face ; his nerves all slacked,
He groaned, then reeled with quick convulsive
    start—
His heart was broke' ; his "dear sweet love" was
    lost —
And, falling, tolled his own death-knell which
    cracked
The engine bell — "the bell of the broken heart."

FRIENDSHIP.

Fresh nature has her countless charms,
   And charms which fill our heart with pleasure ;
Yet all her charms are poor compared
   With those we *feel :* the heart's warm treasure.

The woods and hills and lakes and rills,
   The ferns and flow'rs and April showers,
The songs of birds with all their trills
   Can ne'er compete with hearts, all ours.

There is a charm in friendship dear,
   With which there's naught on earth comparing ;
The look, the touch, the word of cheer,
   The gentle confidence and trusting.

CHARLES BRADLAUGH.

Charles Bradlaugh ! never more sacred name
E'er spelled, in burning letters, on the shrine
Of truth ; clear and consistent it shall shine —
Eternal light within the halls of Fame.
The very name of Hoxton now recalls
Thy birth, the early struggles of thy life
Encompassed 'round by seas of dearth and strife
The like of which our lot scarce e'er befalls.
Mart. Luther sinks beneath thee in reform ;
Thy life is now a shining monument of light —
A paragon of virtue — guide for youth.
"*Iconoclast*" abreast the threat'ning storm
Rides o'er the waves, perforce of manhood's might
And illustrates again the power of Truth.

'NEATH THE SHADOW OF THE LINDEN.

'Neath the shadow of the linden
   'Neath its broad protecting arms,
I have lived snug days of winter,
   I have bathed in summer charms.

I have breathed the breath of morning
   There have felt the evening dew
And have dreamed beneath its branches
   All the long, lone day through.

There the stars have spun me legends,
   And the warm sou' wind, sweet lays ;
There the soft, deep shades of evening
   Have whispered of other days.

And there the dear echo-voices
   Of departed ones I hear ;
Again the multitudinous silence
   Half fills my heart with fear.

"*There the stars have spun me legends*
And the warm sou' wind, sweet lays."

And there the ghost-like train of fancies
   Through my vision lightly roves ;
Come and go in silent numbers
   All my early dreams and loves.

And the dear old tree, the linden,
   That stands beside my door,
Has bound my heart in its branches
   With days that come no more.

Bound and twined within its branches,
   Ghosts of dreams that are no more,
And the dear sweet forms and faces
   Of loved ones gone before.

So I love the tall old linden
   With its dark and solemn leaves,
And its deep heart rustling over
   Once my humble cottage eaves.

ICONOCLASTIC RHYME.

DEDICATED TO THE ULSTER COUNTY SUNDAY SCHOOL ASSOCIATION.

The world is still deceived with ornament.
In law, what plea so tainted and corrupt,
But being season'd with a gracious voice
Obscures the show of evil? In religion,
What damned error, but some sober brow
Will bless it, and approve it with a text,
Hiding the grossness with fair ornament.

SHAKESPEARE.

Conditions and Environment
Gave birth to race and government ;
But Herod-Prejudice, with scorn,
Declares "the 'blacks' ought not been born ;
But since they *are*, the heinous 'crime'
Deserves the lash of ev'ry clime."

In days of yore they lashed the slaves
With thongs of hide — the heartless knaves —
Nor vanished are those cruel days :
They lash them yet in other ways : —

Good men and women ostracised
By brutes, 'neath custom, long disguised;
By members of some other race,
Whose only worth, a paler face,
Believe by that and through God's grace
In heaven to find some better place
Than He accords the Afric race.
O, Ignorance, thou heartless brute!
By Superstition bred, and sired ·
By Prejudice — of Hell desired —
Thou hast but one string to thy lute:
The low-bred chord of selfishness
Whose only tune is: " Wretchedness
To all the world save me — and — well —
Give me my fill of selfish love
And when I die, O, God above!
Save *me* though millions go to Hell.
Give me a golden harp to play
With Heav'nly songs of Thine to sing
Beside some crystal, flowing spring,
Then I will make the welkin ring
While Hell roars hot with fires to flay
Poor devils not so fortunate;
In *virtue's* law perhaps who lack
A paler face — God damn the black! —

But *bless* us, Thy elective great,
As we do crown thy old gray pate,
With prayers and lies and flattery
And heartless, vile hypocrisy.

I know I am a 'weakly worm'
And laugh to see poor wretches squirm,
While piling high the sticks to burn
The devilish heretics who spurn
That sacred lie — Thy Holy Book
That teaches us of witch and spook ;
Defiles the race of womanhood
And tells us that 'tis grand and good
To strike her down with cruel stones,
And bruise her flesh and break her bones ;
Because she *dares* to want to know
A thing or two, give her a blow.

And how I'll laugh when Ingersoll
Drops off the world down into Hell,
For teaching men the sacredness
Of human love, the blessedness
Of womanhood, and constancy,
And all his good philosophy.
For daring to teach common sense
We'll give him Hell as recompense,

And burn him by the side of Paine
And laugh to hear him call for rain
To cool the fever of his tongue,
The fire of which, then scarce begun,
Shall burn through all Eternity —
By will of God's Divinity —
God bless *us* all, Amen !"

THE MINER'S DREAM.

'Twas late one summer afternoon,
   The sun had almost set ;
The West had scattered all her hues
   Upon the rain-clouds wet.
Far back within a wilderness
   Beside a cabin door,
An agèd man, gray bearded, rough,
   Lay sprawled upon the floor.

His dress was that the miners wore
   Some forty years ago ;
Uncouth, unkempt, he pufft·his pipe,
   His hair was white as snow ;
His chin he rested on his hand·
   His elbow on the floor,
While gazing at the setting sun
   The blue smoke wreathed his door.

His eye was fast upon the clouds,
   Though not a cloud he saw ;
His mind was wand'ring back again
   Perforce of Nature's law,

To days gone by, yet close to him,
  In dreams and mem'ry near ;
And songs were sung and voices rung
  Familiar to his ear.

He saw once more the cherished past,
  Dream-peopled as of yore ;
And saw the camp-fire's distant glow
  Which shone like yellow ore.
Loud peals of laughter from the gorge
  Bespoke that wit went 'round,
Though clad in rough and homely garb
  'Twas rich with merry sound.

The winding line of miners by
  The river's ruffled edge,
Are panning out their "ounce a day,"
  Are delving in the ledge.
The streams once more run clear and cold —
  Sierra's liquid snow —
And wander down their natural beds
  With no impeded flow.

He sees the dreams that Harte has sung,
  Recalls them to his mind ;
They come to him from ghosts of trees,
  In voices of the wind ;

They stand out from the vanished past
    In clear and bold relief,
Congealing all his mental pow'rs
    In his one sad belief :

That from the West all glory fled
    With civilizations' sweep ;
Where once was wild with pine and oak —
    A forest dark and deep —
Now scattered o'er with homes of men
    And cultivated field,
Which only *tame* facilities
    To labor offer yield.

And all beneath his *dignity*
    A " forty-niner " proud —
To till the fields or herd the flock
    Or mingle with the crowd.
A man of pessimistic view,
    Yet one of a mighty race
Whose sole developed mental trait
    " Is slightly off its base."

INTER NOS.

O, if I could tell all my heart feels, love,
   All the joys to me you've given ;
O, if I could paint with words, love,
   Our wing-foot'd days of heaven,
I'd blend the stillness of a spring-tide eve
   With the closing song of a summer night,
And hush the moon-beams on the sloping eave
   With the music of mid-winter star-light ;
      And I'd sing thee a song
      Of love sweet and long
    In a sleepy little village,
      In a little white cot :
    In a vine-clad cottage by the wall,
    Where a charming little woman
      In a little white cot,
    In a dream-nest-bower by the wall,
      Lives and loves me very well
      And she calls me " Papa Bell "
    Through the love-lit* lattice near the fall.

Lit may not be very elegant, but it serves the purpose well.

WAKE LOVE.

O wake, wake, wake love, and ope thy lattice wide;
The dawn is breaking on the world, the lonesome
    night has died;
The owl has fled to dark retreats, the night bat
    roams no more,
O come from out thy resting place and ope thy
    lattice door.

O wake, wake, wake love, the sun half o'er the hill,
Is gilding all the mountain tops and paints your
    window sill;
The dew is on the clover bloom, the wild flow'rs
    scent the air,
The morn is rich, the morn is fresh, but thou alone
    art fair.

O wake, wake, wake love, and see the day-god rise,
For not a star in all the sky dare look thee in thine
    eyes;
O come from out thy resting place and walk a
    while with me
Up yonder hill to look upon the dawn's broad-
    bosomed sea.

So wake, wake, wake love, and ope thy lattice wide ;
Breathe deep the Morning's fragrant breath and be
    the Morning's bride ;
The dew is on the clover bloom, the wild flow'rs
    scent the air,
The morn is rich, the morn is fresh, but thou alone
    art fair.

TO MAMY.

Of all the joys this earth can give
    There's none to me so sweet and mild,
So free from guile, so pure and true
    As the budding love of a little child.

FAREWELL TO ULSTER.

*To members of the Kingston Bar, with great respect I
dedicate this unassuming verse.*

The dreaded time approaches near
When I must wander far from here,
But ere I start, a trembling. tear
I pause to drop with aching fear
Upon the sward o' my youth's green grave ;
Then breast the ocean's crested wave,
The storms of life, how e'er they rave,
To seek the goal, I, yearning, crave.

No more I'll roam these rugged hills,
No more I'll taste these dancing rills,
Nor seek the precious metals here
Which in the Shawangunk's oft appear ;
No more I'll land the speckled trout,
Nor woods resound my gladsome shout —
Leave all, and foreign dangers dare ;
To fill my purse my heart must tear.

Nor fear I most the billows' roar,
Nor fear a death on foreign shore,

But loath to break the ties that bound
My youthful days to hallow'd ground;
And oft will long to hear the sound
My mountain streams make coursing down;
And for the mid-day hum in town
When Autumn hills are bare and brown.

Hills of pain and dells of pleasure —
   Scenes my wretchedness renew —
Years of pain and months of pleasure,
   Now a long, heart-felt adieu.

Silver Rondout calmly flowing
   Through the scented clover bloom,
Fare thee well, for I am going
   To my fortune or my tomb.

Fare thee well, small vine-clad cottage,
   Where I wooed my own true love.
Fare thee well, dear bow'rs of pleasure
   Where my love first found his love.

Fare thee well! my dear old birth place,
   Torn by Greed of Gain from me;
Fare thee well; my dear old hearth place,
   Oft I'll long and mourn for thee.

Fare thee well ! to birds and flowers,
   I must ever from them part ;
Fare thee well ! fresh skies and showers
   Thou shalt ever have my heart.

Friends that in my mem'ry ever
   Gratitude holds near and dear,
Fare thee well ! and bless you ever !
   I shall miss your words of cheer.

Hills of pain and dells of pleasure —
   Scenes my wretchedness renew.
Years of pain and months of pleasure,
   Now a long heart-felt adieu.

Ye sages of the Kingston Bar,
   Ye men of learning, heart and truth,
Ye warriors proud, with many a scar
   To mark the battles of your youth,
Ye brave, heroic noblemen,
   "Ye favor'd, ye enlightened few,"
Ye versed in "points" above the ken
   Of countrymen, my lords, adieu !

Oft have we met at Johnson's *bar*
   And quaffed his wine with great delight,

And oft to view the Polar Star
   We braced the lamp-post half the night ;
And oft around " *The's* " festive board
   At dominoes we'd sit and play ;
To cure the *grip* we inward poured
   His " rock and rye " 'til break of day.

But Time, the tragic actor, plays
   Unerring lines of pain and mirth
That run throughout our nights and days
   Bankrupting all upon the earth,
Save *one :* our *honest* " Billy " —
   Who grasps old Time by forelock hoar
Nor will release until he pays
   Poor " Billy's " debts, or grants him more.

Then fare thee well, my idols dear —
   Ye members of the Kingston Bar —
In leaving you forgive the tear
   I drop when going off so far ;
And one request is all I ask :
   When meet ye at our Johnson's *bar*
And nightly tip the amber flask,
   Recall to mind your friend afar.

Farewell! old Ulster's dreamy vales,
Her woods and streams and hills and dales;
The scenes of all my early loves,
The scenes where still my fancy roves;
The still retreats of coot and hern
And lowland brooks, thick hedged with fern,
"Farewell my friends! farewell my foes;"
My heart with *these!* to hell with *those.*

Lightning Source UK Ltd.
Milton Keynes UK
UKHW012335061118
331891UK00010B/848/P